INTRODUCTION

GOOD OMENS FOR OLD DOGS

Recently our neighbors brought their new puppy home from the breeder. They had waited a long time for Lucas and had looked forward with great anticipation to his arrival. They had read books and purchased a dog bed, leashes, collars, bowls, brush, and comb.

puppy or will she love him? Where does one walk a dog? And so on . When cute, young Lucas arrived he would be the center of his family's attention, that's for sure.

When you look around at dog training sites and dog shows, youth also takes precedence. Five, six, or seven-year-old dogs appear much less in public. You may see them

Older dogs are usually more loving, less mischievous and develop personalities more like their owners.

We, the neighbors with dog experience, were grilled endlessly— what food is good, where do you buy it, what may he eat, how much? Did we know a good veterinarian? Will the puppy run away, will he crawl under the fence? Will our other dog bite the

occasionally at trials or shows, but these professional athletes and showmen, who are in their best years, constitute an infinitesimal minority.

When I was first asked if I might be interested in writing about the old dog, I was at first surprised.

Who would care about this topic, I thought. Then, when I started talking about it to the dog people among my acquaintances, almost everyone was enthusiastic about the project. The reasons were many. Our attitude toward our dogs has changed. We take our canine friends very seriously. We make ourselves knowledgeable by means of books and, today, have recourse to a very large body of insights into canine behavior.

Life expectancy of our dogs is rising due to improved preventive health care and improved medical attention.

Our dogs' old age is less beset by ailments than in the past. Veterinary medicine has accumulated a large body of knowledge about older dogs. Soon there will be veterinarians and clinics specializing in geriatric care, just as is the case in human medicine.

Many responsible dog owners want to be as informed as possible about each stage in their dogs' lives so that they provide the best possible care for their dogs. Thus, thinking about our canine friend does not stop once he is well-trained or when he no longer requires our constant supervision. Every stage in a dog's life is interesting, has its special attraction, requires its own form of

health care, and requires new tasks and inventive imagination on our part. It is a good omen that the old dog has become a topic of conversation in dog clubs and among dog fanciers.

Basically, it is the same for dogs as it is for humans. If we are doing well, then our trusty canine friends should also be doing well. Our changed attitude toward our own old age is transferred to our dogs. This, too, is a good omen for the old dog.

If you have heard bad stories about the suffering of old dogs, these are the exception. Dogs definitely age with less problems than most humans do. This is one reason why this book has not been written by a veterinarian. Aging, especially the aging of dogs, is not a disease.

Old age is an interesting, important part of life. Old age is the time when the dog owner harvests, so to speak, the results of a long-lasting process. Almost all dogs improve with age, so look forward to it. You have every reason to be proud of your old chap because, hopefully, he has grown old gracefully in your home and with you. I hope that this little book will prepare you in a positive way for this phase in your relationship with your dog and may provide you with some useful pointers.

GROWING OLD

Friendship with a dog is something wonderful. Clearly we all wish that we will be able to enjoy it as long as possible. While we understand that he will grow old, we are afraid of him actually *being* old. Why? Veterinarians tell humans, dogs do not become senile. Dogs are not afraid of growing old. So what are we afraid of when we think about his old age?

In earlier days when people had dogs primarily for their

As dogs get older, like humans, some of the bodily functions change a bit. The slowing down results in less eating, which means less need for toilet relief.

us that dogs age relatively free of problems. As they get older, they do everything a bit more slowly. They do not jump up immediately, but seem to deliberate whether or not the neighbor's cat is worth the effort of a chase. Their energy and strength diminish, they take longer rests, and they need more sleep. Some bodily functions change or are no longer as reliable as they used to be. But, unlike usefulness, not much time or thought was wasted on a flock guardian or hunting dog that was no longer able to work. In most cases, a gunshot ended the working life of a utility dog, and if it should happen that an owner put his old dog to pasture, he was often considered a sentimental fool.

In earlier times, dogs were hardly ever allowed to grow old.

Inability to work, minor deterioration of health, or diminishing ability to react, became death sentences. Today, we have dogs mostly as companions and partners. We establish close and loving relationships with them. For an average dog lover, it is unimaginable that he would have his dog killed just because the dog is old.

Nowadays, our dogs are expected to grow old. But be old? Because we have accepted dogs so intimately into our company, we tend to anthropomorphize them, or think of them as people. Our worries about their aging are shaped by our attitude to our own aging. The position of the elderly in society is in constant flux. Those periods in the history of human civilization when old age was respected were few in number, at least if we study practices rather than ideologies. Where reverence and respect were shown, it was almost always for the old ones' superior knowledge, experience, and what used to be called wisdom.

Nowadays, knowledge changes more quickly than a person can keep up with, and the young possess more valuable knowledge and experience is thought of as a hindrance to progress.

The elderly are desirable members of society as long as they are consumers. The active senior who keeps buying new clothes, goes on excursions and tours, purchases new cars, participates in sports, etc., is well regarded. In the media or in public, old age either does not take place at all or it is glorified.

Our modern attitude toward old age is difficult and often beset by worries about physical ailments, mental disintegration, being declared incompetent, and much more. Rarely is old age seen as something beautiful, interesting, or meaningful. All of these sentiments are transferred to our old canine friend because we have formed such a strong attachment to him.

Here, as in many other instances, anthropomorphizing is the wrong thing to do. It would be better if we learned from our friend rather than seeing him as another human being. He just grows older. He feels changes in himself and adjusts to them. He adjusts without any great ideological fuss. As his physical conditions change, he makes his life as comfortable and cozy as he can, and strives for maximum well-being.

As humans we have the advantage over our dog in that we are able to anticipate and to prepare ourselves. We are able to take precautions and, in a number of areas, even preventative actions. We should make use of this advantage both in our own and in the dog's interest.

HOW LONG WILL HE LIVE?

Nobody can tell you how old your dog will get. Sure, we know that small dogs generally live longer than large dogs. Bitches will generally live longer than males. Dogs that must live outside usually do not grow as old as those dogs that live with us inside the house. These are only rules of thumb.

This boxer is older than his master! Children must be taught to respect the older dog.

An old beagle whose face is almost completely grey.

There is always the chance that the individual dog will outlive the life expectancy of his particular breed or that he will not even get close to it.

Veterinarians with whom I spoke started with the premise that more dogs reach an older age today than did in the past due to better knowledge among owners and in veterinary medicine. We will gladly believe this and hope that it is true for the sake of our dogs.

HOW OLD IS MY DOG?

I am sure you are familiar with the old equation in which one dog year equals seven human years. Today this equation is no longer believed to be valid. At any time, your dog is at a state of his development that applies only to him and cannot be read from any table. If we watch the "veterans' class" at a dog show, that is, dogs eight years and up, we see enormous differences in vitality even among dogs of the same breed.

WHEN WILL MY DOG BE OLD?

If your dog inherited the proper genetic package and if he is healthy, you will hardly notice the onset of aging. There will be indications, but no real ailments. As with humans, graying is a sign of old age, and there are individual dogs whose hair turns gray at a relatively young age. The graying starts first at the chin, then the muzzle. Especially with blond, red, or brown dogs, the head turns sometimes completely white. The skin thickens and loses elasticity. Molting is no longer as dramatic as it used to be and the coat as a whole is no longer as luxuriant.

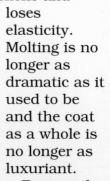

An old dachshund. Old is a relative term. Many very large dogs only live to 5-6 years of age. Small dogs, like this one, can live twice as long.

Frequently, the eyes become more opaque. There may be hearing loss. The sense of smell, however, appears never to lessen. And since he is a "nose animal" it does not bother him all that much if sight and hearing no longer function quite as precisely as they used to.

He will jump up on the couch less frequently and may stop playing with his ball; may avoid climbing stairs, unless it is absolutely necessary; stretches longer and more often; gets up more heavily; and must take a few steps before the stiffness leaves his body.

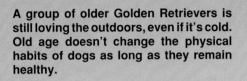

A group of older Golden Retrievers is still loving the outdoors, even if it's cold. Old age doesn't change the physical habits of dogs as long as they remain healthy.

Along with the reduced exercise comes a decrease in the amount of food needed.. Old dogs will become fat if their owners ignore this decrease in the food requirement.

The teeth may cause problems by becoming loose, or because of an increased susceptibility to tartar as concomitant gum infections arise. The toenails will grow longer because he moves around less, and his muscles no longer feel quite as strong and hard. His reflexes will slow down as

well. We can easily miss this development. But we should watch out for it because it may require us to become more attentive and protective.

Studies have shown that one-quarter of all nine- to twelve-year-old dogs suffer from heart disease; thus, the circulatory system becomes less able to cope with stress.

The liver and pancreas can cause problems, and occurrences of diabetes increase in dogs over eight years of age. The body's own immune system grows weaker and the risks of tumors increase.

It is possible that your dog will develop problems with incontinence. If your veterinarian cannot help, simply overlook the accidents just as you did when he was still a pup. The excretory work of the kidneys decreases with age. There will be a larger proportion of waste products in the blood plasma.

In some dogs these changes are hardly noticeable. Others suffer great distress as they age. What ailments, if any, your dog will acquire you cannot foresee, but you can resolve to participate in your dog's old age with dignity, love, respect, and friendship—and then you will both be okay!

OLD DOG, DREAM DOG

No more rabbit chasing

The Schröders are very proud of their two-year-old retriever. "Our Corro is coming along beautifully," they said. "He almost always obeys, unless he sees a cat or a rabbit ahead." I smile indulgently, ruffle my Andra's head, and say with self-content, "Andra no longer chases things." Andra basks in the admiration that is coming her way and I bask right along with her, because, after all, it has been my persistent, expert, and crafty training that has produced this paragon of a dog.

And, indeed, it is true. Lately I have been observing that Andra appears somewhat peeved and looks away whenever she spots a rabbit. It is quite obvious that she does not want to see the prey. It does not interest her. After having a number of bad experiences with unsuccessful hunting efforts, older dogs will calculate their chances very closely. Rabbits become less interesting. Experience, not man's

Older dogs develop a solemn, serene sweet beauty that is not visible in young puppies.

pedagogic effort, produces this exemplary behavior.

Thus, the reference to Andra's loss of interest in chasing rabbits was perfect as the heading for this chapter. It is always true that your old dog has accumulated a lot of experiences. Experiences with hunting, automobiles, children, strangers, neighbors, veterinarians, the farmer's dog and the lap dog of Miss Touch-Me-Not, mice, cats, stairs, carpets and tiles, and dog school. And he has evaluated all the experiences of his canine life by the only two criteria that a dog can: Is it good for me or is it not good for me? That is why his human companion no longer needs to be on guard constantly — he has become smart. And because your senior has this inexhaustible wealth of experiences, he is an absolute dream dog for you. If your dog is still an obstreperous young fellow, you may look forward to his old age with anticipation.

LIVING IN HARMONY

Any dog owner has a plethora of stories to tell how reasonable and highly intelligent his dog is. He knows exactly when his mistress will leave for the office or to go grocery shopping—he knows it, of course, even before the coat closet is opened. Even if there is no such canine superbrain at the end of your leash, all dogs know the members of their pack and their individual habits—both the good ones and the bad ones—and arrange their behavior accordingly.

The dog knows that a yearning look will always get his way with the master. The master will put on his tennis shoes and take the dog for a walk, and it is always good for a treat. He knows that, with the mistress, other things are required. He uses a look that indicates that there is need for great hurry and an accident is imminent unless the mistress slips quickly into her windbreaker. Andra, for example, knows exactly when it is Sunday. Obviously, she does not know what Sunday is, but she knows exactly—-and shows it through her exceptionally good mood—that there is one wonderful day in the week that begins with her people sleeping in, with elaborate breakfast preparations, and, finally, with her weekly dog biscuit.

Your dog knows when you leave for work, go grocery shopping, leave for the theater, or go to visit friends. Disgruntled, the dog will evaluate the clothes you've selected, and from this draw correct conclusions about what's going to happen next.

Allegedly, master/mistress and dog will start to resemble each other more and more as their life together takes its course. And I am sure you know at least one couple that confirms this theory. For instance, there is a neighbor and his dog, Waldo, who march in sync through the village. There is the venomous woman down the street who vents her anger at the slightest provocation noisily, supported by her dog. Or there is my Andra who is a passionate lover of desk work (by me) and identifies immediately a desk chair or garden bench as the beginning of a nice comfortable rest period (for her). We have grown so accustomed to each other that we live in harmony.

If you have not committed any serious mistakes, your dog will have unshakable trust in you and you almost the same in him. He will not suffer a nervous breakdown whenever you leave the house to do your errands. He observes all these incomprehensible human activities with equanimity because he feels safe in your affection and love. You know your old friend through and through. You know when you need to keep an eye on him and when you can allow him freedom. Your old dog follows you everywhere out of good shared experiences. And you, you won't mind following your old friend occasionally on some crooked ways because you have no longer to prove anything. The rank order between the two of you has been clearly established, hopefully in your favor.

Any age in the life of a dog has its special attraction, and old age possesses a special magic. When I yawn, Andra yawns, and the other way around. I notice in me a strong impulse to yawn whenever Andra is tired. You all know the imperceptible stimuli to which our dogs react. That is why they "understand" us so well.

An old Irish Setter.

We as owners have also learned during our shared life. I know if my dog feels well or not, when he wants to be petted or left alone. One glance is enough. Such wordless understanding is rare between people. A relationship with a dog can be great practice because, among ourselves, we rely almost exclusively on the spoken word, and that can be deceiving.

Do you still remember how the puppy changed your life in a friendly but determined way when you brought him into your home? Think of the strenuous, funny, frustrating, and often unsuccessful efforts to turn him into a civilized housemate. Nowadays, he no longer requires our constant efforts to teach him. That does not mean that boredom has set in, but rather that your life together has reached a higher plateau.

Dog and man have come to an arrangement. This word is usually used in a derogatory sense, but here it is meant very much as a positive statement. This mutual arrangement can be disturbed only by you. Your dog is incapable of doing so. He will always be loyal and that is how our relationships with dogs differ from our partnerships with people. That is the reason why many people prefer a friendship with a dog to the love of a person. Certainly, this is not right, but we should not criticize the person that has been hurt in the past; rather, we should encourage people to deal with each other in such a way that friendship with a dog is a supplement to, not a substitute for, a rewarding relationship between people.

OLD DOGS, NEW TRICKS

Many people still believe the outdated theory that learning stops at a given age is true when referring to our four-legged friends. In fact, things are pretty much the same with dogs as they are with people.

LIVING IS LEARNING

The wild ancestors of our housemates had difficult lives. Hunting was a severe test of intelligence for the wild wolves and wild dogs. Mother Nature, however, had equipped her children with various talents that made their difficult lives easier. To begin with, nature left the area of "instinctive"

behavior comparatively small. Only a few things in the life of a wolf proceed according to predetermined patterns, i.e., inborn, automatic, without the individual animal itself knowing what it is doing.

Your dog's wild ancestors had to adjust to ever-changing hunting grounds, so they had to forever discover and try new animals and plants for food. Thus, nature gave wolves and dogs a large void that they had to

fill through learning. Obviously, this is more strenuous than if everything were predetermined. It also makes our friends "smarter" than other animals because they are capable of adjusting to unfamiliar situations on their own and of learning from experience. This means that our dogs are animals with the pronounced ability to learn, to evaluate experiences, and to change behavior. For survival in the wild, our dogs' ancestors were additionally given the ability to cooperate with each other in the pack, immensely improving the chances of making a kill. For this cooperation to bring about results, the wolves or dogs needed the ability to communicate with each other.

Dogs' great ability to learn, their inborn desire for the security and companionship of the pack, and their readiness to communicate are the three talents that, to this day, make possible the wonderful relationship between man and dog. In the context of this book, it is important to remember that this ability to learn new things does not disappear at any given point. However, one can cease to learn entirely (this we know to be true for people), or learn only occasionally and, as a result, become slower to absorb new data. This is also true for our dogs. A dog who is continually challenged, who is given (new) tasks all the time, and who lives in active interchange with his environment and his people will continue to learn to the last moment of his life.

The old saying that "idleness brings rust" is especially true for learning. Exercising one's brain is an absolute must not only for people but also for dogs in the pursuit of an active, interesting, and happy life.

GAMES MAKE CLEVER DOGS

Play games and invent games to play with your old dog. You are the one who knows what he can still do both physically and mentally, so taking this into account, challenge him. Allow for his increased need for rest and his limited mobility, and start planning. Expand the search games that he knows already and if he should indeed not know any, teach your old dog new tricks. Make him search for various objects in your house. Send him to find a hidden person or play hide-and-seek with him yourself. He will learn it quickly and enjoy it. Lay a trail for him at the end of which a surprise (treat) is waiting for him. On your walk, "lose" an item and send him to look for it.

To do this, the dog needs smarts, but not necessarily the best possible physical conditioning. Searching and finding are some of the most enjoyable activities for our dogs. You can also play hide-and-seek with enthusiasm no matter how old your dog.

Play games of fetch with your dog. Teach her the names of a number of items and ask her to bring them. Andra owns a number of different stuffed animals, barbells made of fabric, and other assorted toys, all stored in a box. Whenever she is in the mood to play, she will always bring the toy that I want her to bring. Almost all dogs like to fetch and will do so reliably if we teach them without force and make it an enjoyable experience for them. Send your dog with the mail, the newspaper, clean socks, or other important items as the "official messenger" to various members of the family.

There are no limits to your imagination when inventing and developing tasks. It will be fun for both of you and you will garner a lot of admiration when your dog, upon a slight signal, fetches the television guide from the magazine basket. Practice "language tricks" with your dog. "Sing" a song together. Demonstrate that your dog knows how to "count." Teach him to bark on a hidden hand signal. This trick can be modified and refined in many ways.

Invent short "dog sketches" or acts. Here, too, there are no limits to your imagination. For instance, you could teach your dog to do exactly the opposite of what you

ask her to do. Teach her to play the very angry dog or to "die" laughing. Simply try to remember all those dog tricks that you have seen in the circus or on television and copy them. It will be good for your dog, and for you as well, because you must use your head and figure out the easiest way for your special dog to learn special tricks. Don't be embarrassed. Rather, take your cue from the fact that allegedly "useless" game-playing is one of the favorite and most valuable cultural activities—not only in the world of man.

Enjoy the games you play with your oldie and keep inventing new ones. Teach games and tricks to your dog and both of you will be proud beyond measure whenever a new trick goes off as planned. Challenge his brain and your own, and your senior will grow old happier and surely healthier as well.

This old Collie mix still retrieves from the water.

This black Cocker Spaniel has developed a white beard,

Aging is not a disease, neither for dogs nor for humans. Modern medicines have done much to help a dog live its full, complete life.

CARE FOR THE AGING DOG

AGING IS NOT A DISEASE

Anyone who has spent some time in a veterinarian's waiting room is familiar with the nervous, worried faces of people with sick dogs. Others may make fun of these people but you can certainly understand their feelings. Dogs occupy an important place in the lives of their owners, and the fact that owners worry about the health of their dogs is one manifestation of this importance.

In earlier times, veterinary surgeons frequently advised against surgical procedures for older dogs. Nowadays, veterinary medicine has made sufficient advances so that, in most cases, surgery on older patients is no longer a problem. And today most dog owners will not be deterred by the costs that are involved with surgery.

I have been noticing that this is my own attitude. With each dog, medical care became more advanced, and my awareness of possible health disorders more acute. Canine seniors also profit from our increased sensitivity towards matters of health. Old age in itself is not a disease, but it is true that prevention of health problems is the best medicine.

If your dog should age suddenly and visibly, it will, most likely, be a case of an overwhelming health disorder rather than old age alone. Observe your dog, exercise him properly, feed him sensibly, and enjoy your life together, and old age should not present any great problems to your dog.

The old dog has become part of your life, a part taken so for granted that danger arises if you no longer observe him all that closely. But that is exactly what your old dog needs most. An old dog is being neglected if he is not paid the attention that has now become necessary.

The following pages provide information about the most important age-related ailments that befall dogs. Keep in mind that your dog, most assuredly, will not get all these ailments, and may not show any noticeable signs of any of these diseases. Old age is not exactly an easy time for people or dogs. Making light of it or glorifying it is no help, neither is over-dramatization. The information presented here is meant to sharpen your awareness. It is not a substitute for a visit to the veterinarian, nor is it meant to frighten you.

WHAT MAY AIL YOUR OLD DOG

Musculoskeletal System

Things happen to dogs very much the way they happen to us. When dogs get older, they "feel their bones." Moving around no longer comes easily. Getting up, especially after they have been lying for a while, is hard, and sometimes it looks as if the old fellows need to take a few steps before their movements become smooth again.

Many dogs have problems with their intervertebral discs and the wear on these joints becomes more and more painful. The muscles are no longer capable of counteracting many of these difficulties because dogs, just as people, lose muscle as they age. This is clearly visible in very old dogs in the prominent spines of the thoracic vertebrae. The abdominal wall appears more flaccid and the upper thighs are withered.

When you notice that your dog "feels his bones," has difficulty getting up, is lame, and no longer jumps onto the couch with enthusiasm, then go and see your veterinarian. He won't be able to stop the aging, but he can offer supportive and alleviating treatment for a number of ailments and slow down the aging process through preventive measures. Do not wait too long.

You can help by making sure that your dog is always slightly underweight—a difficult task! Take him on several short walks throughout the day rather than on one or two long ones. Watch

out that he does not overdo it when playing or working. Most importantly, he should be protected against humidity, cold, and dampness and have a dry, soft bed.

Heart and Circulatory System

The canine heart is a muscle capable of bearing great stress and designed for much larger demands than life usually places on it. The heart has sufficient reserves to work satisfactorily even under very stressful conditions.

This muscle loses elasticity through the years without our noticing. A heart weakness or insufficiency may occur. Dogs with weak hearts will tire much faster and no longer tolerate stresses that did not bother them at all before. They will become short of breath and, lastly, show the well-known "heart cough" even with slight exertion.

The veterinarian can help if you react quickly to these symptoms. If we pay attention to our dog's ailment and give him his medicine regularly, he will usually be able to lead a normal life. If you ignore these symptoms, his heart will worsen to the extent that it will no longer be able to keep the circulation going sufficiently to provide all organs of the body with enough oxygen. When this happens, circulatory collapse will become a real threat unless someone intervenes and provides assistance in time.

Many dogs suffer from a valvular defect of the heart that in most cases remains undetected. Naturally, such a defect decreases the effectiveness of the heart, but a canine heart is capable of compensating for a lot.

Because the heart works together with all the other organs, heart disease can negatively affect the efficiency of these other organs. For instance, dogs with heart disease may get lung edema. This happens when insufficient pumping action of the heart causes more fluid to collect in the lungs than can be metabolized. Now, if more and more fluid collects in the lungs, then we hear the cough typical of patients with serious heart disease. Thus, be suspicious whenever your elderly dog coughs—it could be the "heart cough." Elderly dogs can also be susceptible to chronic bronchitis and thus to pneumonia. Coughing is always a reason to visit the veterinarian.

Obviously, medications cannot make a sick heart beat forever. However, if detected in time, the diagnosis "heart disease" does not

mean catastrophe. Your veterinarian will tell you what conditions are best for your dog. Then, you can still enjoy your dog for a long time.

Hormonal System

Older dogs may develop hypothyroidism or hyperactivity of the adrenal glands. Symmetrical loss of hair on the body, in the kidney area, or on the rear legs can be a symptom.

Older dogs, especially bitches, may contract diabetes. The symptoms are similar to those shown by humans: general fatigue, great thirst, vomiting, and if there is no medical intervention, coma and death. Watch out for these symptoms and have your veterinarian run a test.

Unfortunately, there are not yet any pills that will lower the blood sugar level in dogs with diabetes, nor is homeopathy a remedy. You will have to learn to give your dog his insulin injections on a regular basis. Most likely this will be difficult in the beginning and perhaps you will be afraid to do it, but if your dog should indeed contract diabetes you will have to manage to give him his shots. If the disease is diagnosed and treated in time, your dog will still have a few good years ahead of him.

Skin and Coat

Skin problems are more frequent in older dogs than in younger ones. Loss of hair, formation of warts, increased incidents of dandruff, impacted sebaceous glands, and tumors (mostly benign) all can arise.

In earlier times, people used to say that the condition of the coat told a dog's state of health. This is not always true—the skin or coat of a dog is not a sure indicator of overall health. Your veterinarian knows the "whole" dog and will be able to see any skin or coat disease in the context of other observations.

It is always advisable to have warts, sebaceous cysts, and tumors removed. They could become painfully infected if your dog should scratch at them. True, older dogs have, in many cases, lost the luxuriant coats they used to have, but you must continue grooming your dog because there is often a tendency to develop unsightly mats.

Teeth and Gums

It is always astonishing how many old dogs still have great teeth. But here, too, environmental influences may bring deterioration. The best prevention you can offer is to regularly check teeth and gums, provide safe, effective chew devices like Nylabones, which keep plaque at bay, watch for bad breath, and feed your dog sensibly. Brushing the teeth can prevent tartar formation and remove the bacteria that causes bad breath at the same time.

Toothpaste for dogs is available in pet stores.

Tumors

As our dogs grow older, the frequency of tumors increases. The lymphatic system also loses

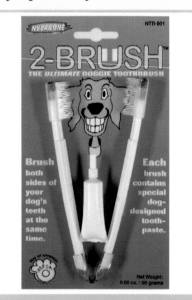

Brushing your dog's teeth, combined with a proper dental chew device, is about as much you can do to help the aging dog keep its teeth. The use of a double brush, which brushes both sides of the teeth at the same time, is better for older dogs than a single brush because brushing with a double brush only takes half as long.

efficiency with increasing age. The body's defenses against disease grow weaker, and benign as well as malignant tumors occur in greater numbers. The diagnosis "cancer" causes great fear, of course, but here too the comparison with people may help. If detected in time, many forms of cancer can be completely eradicated. Together with your veterinarian you can arrive at the proper decision. Remember—most dogs, even if very old, will tolerate surgery, and the results of the surgery are usually excellent. At least let your veterinarian try if he thinks surgery is needed. In many cases the tumors will be benign. Your veterinarian will explain to you if and why such a benign tumor should be removed. You can help best by presenting any growth immediately to your veterinarian.

Genitals

Older bitches often show irregularities in the heat cycle, and connected with this are inflammations and infections of the uterus. The following may be symptoms of metritis: poor general health, excessive thirst, vomiting, and discolored and frequently malodorous discharge. Any of these symptoms may be seen in combination with difficulties in getting up. Older bitches will often develop lumps in their breasts (mammary tumors), especially if they have had many false pregnancies. In both cases, surgery is often the only option.

The typical health problem of the old male is the enlarged prostate. This prostate enlargement can be benign, but it can also be cancerous. In dogs, the prostate is located near the anus. The enlarged prostate compresses the rectum and affected dogs find it difficult to move their bowels. The only early signs are small spots of blood on the dog's bedding after he gets up. It is rare that the urine is entirely colored red.

Either symptom demands an immediate visit to the veterinarian. Castration or regular administration of hormones may help. Your veterinarian will explain what treatment is best for your dog. The best way for you to help is to observe your bitch or dog carefully and not to waste time before consulting your veterinarian.

Urinary System

The kidneys are the large filtering devices of the body. Like the heart, they are designed for enormous work loads. In old dogs, parts of this filtering system are irrevocably used up. There are many causes for kidney diseases, and they may be inconspicuous in the beginning. Chronic illnesses may overtax them.Your old friend may just be a little bit listless. In any case, frequent urination is always a symptom that you should do something about. When your dog no longer can stand on his legs and, due to his chronic kidney disease, falls into a coma, little hope is left.

We speak of kidney failure when the kidneys no longer can excrete the urine-bound constituents and these then poison the body (uremia). If the veterinarian is consulted in time, he often can help.

Many urinary problems are bladder related. In older animals, the bladder is susceptible to a number of different infectious diseases. Watch carefully for any unusual discharge from the vulva or penis because what may begin as a local infection can ascend from the bladder to the kidneys and cause much more serious complications. Dogs can get bladder stones, and the symptoms are the same: discomfort, pain when urinating, and blood in the urine. Your veterinarian can help with surgery. If this is followed with a special lifelong urinary calculus diet, the reoccurrence of bladder stones will be prevented.

Eyes and Ears

The eyes are the windows to the soul, they say, and that certainly is true for our dogs. For the veterinarian, the eyes are frequently the windows through which he may see an illness, since many changes in the body show up in the eyes.

As for older dogs, the eyes seem to grow more opaque with age. Don't worry, this does not mean that blindness is beginning to set in. It is a normal change that occurs in all dogs and usually begins as early as age five or six. We do not know why the lenses of the older dog become clouded. A dog can go blind due to glaucoma or cataracts, two eye diseases of different etiology. A cataract is a clouding of the lens that prevents light from penetrating. Glaucoma is a disorder in the drainage of the fluid inside the anterior eye chamber that causes the pressure inside the eye to increase. Cataracts are more likely to occur in older dogs, but many younger and even very young dogs can be affected by cataracts as well. It has been shown that there is a hereditary predisposition for this disease. There is a hereditary predisposition for glaucoma as well, but usually it has other causes. In either case, under special circumstances surgery by a specialist may be successful.

All dogs lose hearing acuity as they grow older. Frequently we do not even notice it, but we should watch out for it, because this is the time when the dog needs our protection to avoid accidents. Test your dog's hearing from time to time—but not at the very moment when he is chasing a cat, because then he won't hear you for sure. Usually, loss of hearing is a phenomenon of old age with which you and your dog will have to live. With some empathy and by establishing certain routines you will manage to do so. To be on the safe side, discuss the matter with your veterinarian; perhaps there is a different cause for the loss of hearing.

THE IMPORTANCE OF CHECK-UPS

You may have noticed that there are a number of illnesses with similar symptoms. Do not puzzle about possible causes and, above all, do not delay before bringing your dog to your veterinarian, the expert. Hopefully, he will be able to make the correct diagnosis quickly and definitely, and give appropriate treatment. Trust him, and if you cannot bring yourself to do so, change veterinarians at once; for your dog's sake, do not delay.

What follows should be done at all ages but is especially important with an older dog. Check your friend at regular intervals from the tip of his nose to the tip of his tail. See if the nose is smooth and moist, check the clarity (or the degree of cloudiness) of his eyes, and check the condition of the conjunctiva. Inspect and smell his mouth and ears. Test his hearing. Pull up his lips. Tartar likes to form at the neck of the canine and carnassial teeth, even if no other tartar is visible. Check his pads, including the toe pads; they should not be brittle or show cracks. Feel the breasts of your bitch for lumps. Watch for changes in coat or skin and for unusual discharges from the vulva or penis. This quick examination, which you can make part of an enjoyable cuddling session, will provide you with important information about your dog's health. Make the effort, it is worthwhile.

You should already be visiting the veterinarian once a year for the regular check-up and immunizations. If your dog is older than eight, it is advisable to go twice a year for an examination. A very old dog with certain diseases should see the veterinarian even more often than twice a year.

THE VETERINARIAN'S HELPER

Your veterinarian has the problem—some veterinarians call it good fortune—that his patients cannot talk to him and cannot tell him their woes. You must be the intermediary between your dog and the veterinarian. The better you can inform the veterinarian, the better he will be able to treat your dog. This is especially true with older dogs who often have complex, interrelated problems.

However, usually we are so nervous at the veterinarian's that we forget the simplest and most important matters. This is why you should prepare a check-list at home of the most important symptoms that your veterinarian should know about, especially if he is seeing your dog for the first time.

You will see that your careful preparations will make your discussion with the veterinarian much easier. However, it is just as important to follow the veterinarian's instructions properly. This may be a challenge, because our canine friends are quite crafty whenever they wish to avoid unfamiliar handling. Avoid the use of force and make the event as pleasant as possible for your dog.

Usually it is all about administering powders, drops, or pills. If you do it right, your dog will soon insist on getting his medication regularly. My Andra has disc problems. Our veterinarian has ordered homeopathic pills, high doses of vitamin B, and a special food supplement in tablet form. Every morning she gets several pulverized pills, an additional pill wrapped in a piece of cheese and the vitamin pill by itself because she likes it. It is totally impossible for us to forget her morning ration because Andra waits patiently in front of the kitchen cabinet where we keep her medications. It is equally impossible for us to forget one of the remedies, for she will remain sitting until she has indeed received all her medicines.

Her determination in the matter of her medications is a source of great amusement in the family but Andra does not care, her sense of duty in this matter is enormous.

Our male, Ben, was different. No matter how cleverly we disguised his pills, he would always discover them and keep them in his mouth until he could spit them out at the first unguarded moment. We would find the pills under the radiator, on the carpet, under the couch, in the bathroom—everywhere. But even Ben could be tricked—we placed the pill deep in his throat while holding a delicious treat visible in the other hand, and the anticipatory swallow reflex would make the pill disappear. The treat was his deserved dessert. I am sure you, too, will find a right way for your dog. After all, we are the more intelligent beings, aren't we?

Man's age-old yearning for eternal youth helps the makers of lotions, creams, and pills, as well as those who own fat farms and massage clinics. Fortunately, this obsession with youth has not yet affected our dogs. They simply grow old, and that's that. Admittedly, they grow substantially older in human care than they would in the wild. And because this is so, they need a little more attention than they did in their younger years. For instance, there is the matter of the coat. Not until our dog was very old did his coat thin out, which is usually due to hormonal causes. Unlike people, old dogs may grow an even thicker coat. No

The POPpup™ Nylabone® Edible® was made to order for aging dogs. The bone is made of wheat starch with healthful additives like spinach, cheese, chicken, liver, etc. In its natural state it is hard, chewable and satisfying to the dog's need to chew. If it is too hard for your old dog, simply bake it in your microwave oven for about one minute (time varies with size of bone and size of oven). The result is a bread-like mass, eight times its original volume, with a crispy, variable texture.

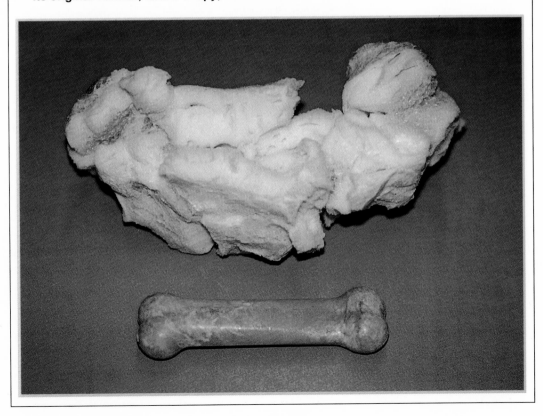

This magnificent Irish Setter, Ch. Quailfield's Mak'N Business, almost 9 years old, won Best of Breed at the Westminster Kennel Club in 1997! Wow!

CHECK UP

Breed of dog		Age	
Gender		Castrated:	Yes/No

Prior Problems

Finding	Inconspicuous	Obvious
General Condition		
Weight		
Nutrition		
Behavior		
Agility		
Coat		
Eyes		
Teeth		
Stomach		
Anus		
Penis		
Testicles		
Vagina		
Temperature		
Gait		
Appetite		
Thirst		
Feces		
Urine		
Vomit		

Symptoms and Abnormalities:

matter your dog's coat type, good grooming is very important as he ages.

Some older dogs become neglectful in their own grooming. This may be caused by general forgetfulness or because the spinal column and the joints have become stiffer and mobility has decreased. In any case, it is advisable to check the penis, vulva, and anus regularly and to clean them whenever necessary. This is not as bad as it sounds, so don't make it into a big deal. Take care of your cuddly dog so that it becomes a pleasant experience for him. With puppies and young dogs, we must grab for a washcloth now and then as they also aren't all that fastidious in personal grooming. At that time you did it with a grin—do it the same way with your oldie! Dogs and people have much in common, including the need for personal grooming.

Canine grannies and grandpas need special foot care. Old dogs no longer run about as much and their walks have become shorter, so the toenails no longer wear on their own. The toenails need to be checked regularly, and, if needed, trimmed (or have them trimmed) and treated with oil whenever they become brittle.

Older dogs are susceptible to tooth problems. Excessive tartar and inflammation of the gums or roots of the teeth are fairly frequent occurrences. Watch for such inflammation, because it is often the point of origin for serious kidney, liver, and even heart diseases. Removal of bad

teeth and treating other tooth problems is routine in the average small-animal practice.

Eyes and ears need your special attention, but you should have been doing that throughout your dog's life. All you need to do in addition for your canine senior is be even more diligent in your attention to these areas.

Old dogs lie around more and calluses at the elbows are the result. Vaseline or similar substances will remedy the situation. Additionally, make sure that his sleeping quarters are well padded, and that you have done nearly everything that you can to guarantee his comfort.

Regular exercise is also part of proper care. As was the case when he was a puppy, we again adjust his exercise to what he is able to do now that he has become a senior. Pay close attention to your old dog. In an attempt to please you, he may overdo it. Take several short walks with him rather than one or two long ones.

Keeping an old dog well groomed and in good health is no great problem if you give him attention and affection. Do not overdo it. Whatever your old friend can do for himself you should not do for him. With your assistance and care he may not necessarily live longer, but he will grow older in better shape and be in more comfort.

SENIOR DIET

The lady next door has a pretty, mid-size mixed breed who is 13 years old. After his morning walk

Struppie gets a bowl of milk soup, at noon he eats part of his mistress' lunch, and for dinner he gets a lard sandwich. Any expert in canine nutrition will shudder at this diet. But not Struppie! Struppie is fit as a fiddle—he has adult animals. Beginning with the seventh or eighth year, however, there are changes in the amount and content that you should know about. As dogs grow older, their bodies can no longer utilize food as well as they used to. Many

As your dog gets older, he might not be able to jump into his favorite chair. You'll have to help him up, as he might struggle to jump onto the chair.

a shiny coat, almost all his teeth, clear eyes, and is in top shape. No reason, then, to worry about a senior diet. All of us know a similar dog, but, unfortunately, they are not the rule. If your senior is not such a wonder dog, it might be advisable to give some thought to a diet that is appropriate for his age.

To begin with, older dogs need the same nutrients as younger oldies have digestive problems because the mobility of their intestines decrease—that, too, is something we are familiar with from our older human friends.

Older dogs need less calories, and you and your veterinarian will need to evaluate what is required for your individual dog. If you continue feeding the usual portions, your skinny dog will turn into a fat matron.

Seniors need considerably more protein, and we should feed them protein of higher quality (e.g., boiled chicken, eggs, fish, cottage cheese). The meat content should not exceed one-third of the total food amount and should contain high-quality, easily digestible protein, such as lean meat and poultry. The remaining two-thirds of the total food amount should consist of easily digestible carbohydrates such as cereals, rice, potatoes, or pasta.

With minerals you must take into account that calcium is now absorbed into the skeleton more slowly and that phosphorus should not be given in excess because of the risk of kidney damage.

There are also changes with the vitamins. Because the liver is no longer capable of storing as much vitamin A as before, and because the water soluble vitamins may be excreted in larger amounts through the kidneys, we must make sure to increase their presence in the food. We proceed with the assumption that the requirement is twice that of the younger adult dog. Have your veterinarian recommend a vitamin/mineral supplement if he thinks your dog needs it.

The dog's sense of taste decreases with age, so make sure

Older dogs can't take too much exercise before they simply stop, lay down and pant. Dogs seldom let you work them harder than they can comfortably perform.

This guy loved the water as a puppy and still loves the water. Some things just don't change with time.

that the food is palatable. Adding a bit of salt or improving the taste with some meat broth not only makes the food taste better but also helps with the age-related kidney problems. Only if your dog has heart disease should the amount of salt be decreased. Older dogs also frequently tend to suffer from constipation. You can help prevent this by adding wheat bran to the food.

The food should be divided into two or three daily portions. This is advisable for younger dogs, but for seniors it is a must. Bones should be forbidden at any age, but this is especially true for the senior.

If you follow the rules, you can prepare the food yourself—most dogs will prefer it that way. The ingredients are fresh, can be selected and checked by you, and usually home-made food is no more expensive than commercial food. However, if you have no desire to become an expert in canine nutrition, almost all brand name producers of dog foods have senior formulations. Talk to your veterinarian, to other dog owners, and to knowledgeable sales personnel about what foods meet your dog's requirements the best.

The general advice with dry food nowadays is to soak the food for at least 20 minutes in water or broth. It appears that eating the food dry is inadvisable for digestion and metabolism at any age, but especially at an old age. It is also a part of adequate nutrition that your senior has plenty to drink.

TRAVELING WITH THE SENIOR DOG

The cruelties that are done to dogs in connection with the vacation travels of their people are common and widespread. Because dogs do not scream loudly, march in demonstrations, write letters of complaint, or go on strike, no one notices their manifold suffering.

Leaving a dog alone is always a great stress on the animal. Sometimes it is unavoidable; for instance, if it becomes suddenly necessary to check into a hospital. In the case of vacation travel, however, this stress can be avoided or kept to a minimum. Frankly, I expect people to either take their dog along or leave him with relatives or friends where the dog already has a second home to which he is accustomed and that he likes. If this is not possible, one simply must not leave on vacation without the dog.

Not every dog is so thick-skinned that he is able to set aside the shock, fear, and sorrow until the next vacation comes around, without developing behavior disorders. Leaving your dog in a boarding kennel or with people who are not members of his pack is, for him, the same as being abandoned or given away. How should he know that you will return?

I think it is our duty and obligation to plan our vacations in such a way that our dog can come along. When we acquired our dog we entered into a contract that says, "You have been entrusted to me and I shall do everything so that you will be happy and grow old in a dignified way befitting a dog." Parking your dog during your vacation is a serious violation of this contract.

Almost all dogs enjoy car rides, and almost all like to go on vacation as long as we do not make traveling miserable for them. Most dogs are totally familiar with travel preparations and, with the first sign of packing, go to great lengths to assure that they are not forgotten. It would be a big disappointment if the old dog was not allowed to come along.

Plan your vacation so you can take your dog along. Traveling is not a problem for older dogs if they have experience in traveling.

The same rules apply to the old dog that applied to the younger one. Select your destination with your oldie in mind. He will probably not be able to tolerate heat and cold as well as he used to. Always have plenty of water available for your senior, and it is advisable to take along a sufficient quantity of his usual food. You should discuss with your veterinarian what to include in your first-aid kit for your four-legged companion. He is familiar with your dog's frailties (if any) and can recommend remedies just in case.

Traveling is absolutely no problem for an older dog if he has done so all his life. We should make some allowances for his age, but it is true that too much caution is often harmful. However, you should discuss it with your veterinarian before you take your old friend on airplane trips. The decision will depend on the individual dog in any case. So, by all means take your old friend with you. If your veterinarian should say that he indeed may not travel anymore, give some thought to vacationing at home for once.

SEX AND THE
SENIOR DOG

THE HEAT GOES ON

Dogs have a positive attitude towards sex. For canine females the sexual engagement is limited to the times of estrus, but there are no such restrictions for canine males.

Unlike people, bitches do not lose their estrus or fertility when they reach a certain age. With many bitches, the intensity of the estrus changes when they become old. In the case of very old bitches we sometimes hardly notice that they are in heat. But this is not necessarily true for your female. Depending on hereditary predisposition, even a very old bitch may be sexually active, interested, and successful. There is no menopause for bitches.

Bessy, our neighbors' bitch, a mixed breed resembling a bobtail, went looking for mates even after she had grown very old. Again and again she found an opportunity to escape from the house. Purposefully she would trot to Robin, our suburban Casanova. Whenever he was not in the street, Bessy would "call" him in a loud and determined voice. Robin would wait patiently for hours for his girl because he was always very well informed about the current "state" of the canine ladies in his territory.

When the two finally found each other, off they ran into the orchards and the fields beyond. They avoided with great cunning and remarkable finesse all search troops sent by their human families. Only after a considerable length of time had passed would they be seen trotting toward home side by side, dirty, exhausted, and peaceful. Fortunately, although the two seemed to love each other very much, they were rather unsuccessful in terms of progeny. Two families were regularly beset by worries during these escapades of the amorous pair. Even though these honeymoon hours remained without tangible results the mutual attraction and interest of the two never wavered until Bessy died at age 12 years, leaving her suitor behind alone.

When our bitch was in season in her younger years, we made the effort to keep her separate, and we must continue to make this effort as when she is older. She still can (and will) engage in sex and become pregnant. By the way, do not trust your old bluestocking—when the right stud comes along, many male-haters can be persuaded. Perhaps she hasn't yet found a suitable male. Such bitches will be especially enthusiastic when their dream dog comes along.

It really should not happen, but if your old girl gets pregnant, hurry to your veterinarian. For surely, he will advise the "after pill." There are a few reasons for this. Accidental litters are undesirable since you are not prepared for the new pups and haven't lined up any homes for them. No litter should be born without an idea of where the pups will go and how they will be taken care of. Also, pregnancy, birthing, and raising pups is not easy for a bitch, especially an old one. To let her have a litter at this age is inconsiderate and could be dangerous. You are the best contraceptive. Keep a watchful eye on your bitch, especially if she is older, and avoid having to make the decision that may be thrust upon you by an unplanned pregnancy.

DON JUAN NEVER RETIRES

My Andra had one especially hot-blooded admirer, Blackie, the black Schnauzer mix. Whenever Andra came into heat, Blackie's mistress was barely able to leave her house. Blackie would drag her with all his might to our place. Sometimes she could not hold on to him. Blackie would tear himself free and race towards Andra. A mighty leap over the fence and then wait patiently until the adored one stepped through the front door. Usually she would not do this because we had been warned over the telephone, but Blackie could at least hope.

Blackie was already elderly when Andra came to us as a puppy. Blackie was quite old when Andra was in her best years. His heart was a cause for worry and his joints hurt. One day, love-crazed Blackie landed once again on Andra's side of the fence and it was his last visit. A short while later he died of a heart attack. You understand the excitement!

Robin, by now quite advanced in age, still runs toward the front door of any bitch in heat in his rather large territory, perhaps not as fast as before but no less determined or self-confident. Old-age ailments, if he even feels them on those days, do not dampen his eagerness to do his duty, and since most of the other males are more strictly confined to their homes, he has hardly any rivals. There is no retirement for a love-crazed stud and we should, in any case, not believe any statements about "becoming calmer with age." Of course, males that were never especially active at the "sex front," will also be calmer when older. Ben, my German Shepherd, was such a dog. He had only a moderate interest in the ladies, but he did have a few bitches that he adored. And, at the advanced age of 11 years, he finally succumbed to the allure of one of these bitches and with notable know-how and tangible results, sacrificed his innocence for her. Possibly, your "Don Juan" will become calmer at

home as he grows older, but don't bank on it.

NEUTERING ELDERLY DOGS

In recent years there has been a lively public discussion among dog fanciers about the pros and cons of neutering dogs. Though it is this author's opinion that if your dog does not have any health problems, there really is no reason why you should have the procedure done, there are many who feel that if you are not going to take the betterment of your breed very seriously, you should not breed your dog. There are also some medical conditions where neutering may be necessary.

Many bitches, especially those who have a tendency to have false pregnancies, are susceptible to uterus inflammations at an advanced age. This is a clear reason for an ovario-hysterectomy. It happened to my Andra. We have not regretted it. She became much more even-tempered because she was freed of all the inconveniences of her estrus, which she took very seriously. She has become a thoroughly happy, good-tempered dog. Those periods of imagined pregnancy during which Andra

There are many discussions among veterinarians and dog owners about spaying or castrating their pets. Obviously, if there is a medical need to castrate or perform an ovario-hysterectomy it should be done. The loss of reproductive ability does not change the dog's personality. It is usual that if a male is castrated when still a puppy, he might continue squatting to urinate like a female.

was always so very tired, hungry and often in a bad mood, are no longer. The excitement of marking is over, often beginning as early as six weeks before the onset of her season, with which Andra wanted to let the world of males know that she would soon be looking for a husband. True, Andra may now become overweight more easily if we do not watch out and her coat has definitely become thicker, but these are things one can live with.

Males are more susceptible to prostate problems if they remain intact, and just as spayed females lose some not-always-pleasant behaviors, so neutered males will not roam, mark or be compulsively territorial. Neutering either sex does not change the personality of your dog; rather, it changes some behaviors.

Perhaps I should also point out, especially for my male readers, that male dogs that have undergone castration have no awareness of a loss. "Castration — yes or no?" is always a question that can be of great importance to your dog for a long, healthy life.

YOUNG AND OLD TOGETHER

When old Senta died, great sorrow filled the house of the Burger family. They missed Senta. The Burgers simply could not live without a dog. Although they knew better, they bought the next best puppy, Janosch, a Kerry Blue Terrier. They were lucky, for Janosch was a splendid dog and brought them much joy.

When Janosch grew old, the Burgers decided that they did not want to go through such great sorrow once again. This time, the successor to Janosch was to be with them ahead of time. Thus, they brought Gora, a young Hovawart bitch, into their home.

From the moment Gora arrived, Janosch ate poorly, withdrew into himself, was depressed, and became moody, even snapping now and then when something displeased him. In this sorrowful state, Janosch spent his last months.

Books on older dogs frequently recommend exactly what the Burgers did. They say the older dog will show the younger dog the ropes. The older dog will be rejuvenated by the younger dog, become more active, and become more interested in the world around him, and when he must pass away, the parting will not hurt as much.

Do not accept this touching recommendation without giving it some thought. It does not apply to all situations or all dogs. The idea that having more than one dog is more appropriate for the canine species is something that your spoiled, single dog won't believe for a minute.

Every dog is different, and what I am going to say now may not be true for your dog. You know your dog well enough to decide for him.

RIVALRY

Perhaps your relationship with your dog is like the one I have with my Andra. We love each other, and she has great respect for and limitless trust in me. We are a well-coordinated team. Andra enjoys clear preference over any other dog among our acquaintances. We spend as much time as possible together. Wherever I am, there is my dog (almost always). I must admit, Andra is spoiled. Why shouldn't she be? She does not bite nor is she in any way neurotic. She is just a happy dog who feels secure and at ease in the affection of her human pack.

I would never impose a second dog upon Andra because I am quite certain that she would suffer. Whatever graciousness Andra extends to visiting dogs only lasts as long as there are reasonable expectations that they will leave

our territory again. It has been a long time since I have taken in another dog to care for because it makes Andra so very unhappy—from the very first to the very last day of the visitor's stay.

A dog who has been the beloved single dog all his life will find it difficult if he is joined by a young dog in his old age. It may work, but this is not probable. Introducing a bitch to an old male has the best chance of success. If he likes her, he will overcome more easily the disappointment

that you and your new young dog have caused him.

The entire matter is more difficult with bitches. If you introduce a puppy into the household, things may go badly for the youngster because bitches don't always treat strange puppies in a motherly fashion. The gestures of submission that usually trigger bite inhibition work automatically only with the bitch's own puppies. Bitches can become aggressive towards strange puppies.

Bitches defend their own litter against the offspring of others, even if they never had puppies. Dog breeders who have been in the position of having to give nursing puppies to a foster mother know this problem. There is a great risk that they will be killed, even though there are many tricks to make the foster mother feel benevolent. The best second dog is the bitch's own puppy, but that is the very thing your old lady (let us hope) can no longer accomplish.

Thus, introducing a puppy into the life of an old single dog is not that easy. What is true for a puppy applies to an even greater extent if you should wish to acquire a younger adult dog. Even if the two dogs have known each other for a long time, it is not at all certain that they will live together peaceably. As a rule, single dogs are not happy with an additional dog in the family. If you, despite this, want to or must offer a home to a second dog, prepare yourself for a comprehensive training regimen. You must make it clear that in your pack only one member sets the rules and this one is you. Of course, you will make sure that your old friend will be top dog, unless he voluntarily surrenders this privilege out of affection for his new foster daughter or lady friend.

Dogs get lonely, but if you bring another dog into your home while the old dog is still around, there could be social problems.

MAY/DECEMBER COMPANIONSHIP

If you and your dog are accustomed to the company of several dogs, then there can be no objection to introducing a young dog to an old dog as long as you take the necessary precautions. The old dog welcomes the company of another dog, which he might have missed, and the young dog will be exceedingly happy to have a dog as model and protector. Puppies are in heaven whenever they find an adult dog in their new home.

Our garden is bordered on one side by the territory of our next-door-neighbor's new puppy, Lucas. Lucas will sit for the longest time at a hole in the hedge and watch our Andra as she performs such instructive tasks as gnawing on twigs, chewing on rawhide, picking blackberries, or guarding our turtle run. Whenever she turns her head slightly in his direction—she knows very well that he is watching her—his body trembles with excitement and his little tail wags furiously.

This hero-worship is indescribable. For Lucas, there is nothing more beautiful than being taken for a walk together with his adored neighbor. Andra, by the way, needs to warn him only once and from then on he will never repeat an undesirable deed. Our human neighbors watch these "training sessions" with undisguised envy. This charming friendship ends, however, as far as Andra is concerned, at our back door. Whenever Lucas shows signs of wanting to come from the garden into the house, Andra intervenes decisively. It is only my voice of authority that can grant Lucas permission to enter.

It is unlikely that older dogs will experience the same joy, but if they are used to the company of other dogs, there should not be many problems. However, in the interest of your senior you should give some thought to the possibility that the young newcomer may physically overtax your old dog. Keep in mind that the new dog, despite all his respect for the older one, may be a wild fellow who could become a danger for your senior. And vice-versa. Your senior, if he should deign to play with the youngster at all, may run over him and seriously hurt him. You must consider and take into account differences in size and strength.

Of course, you might hold to the opinion that the entire problem is silly. In the wild, after

An old Afghan hound. Larger dogs tend to age sooner than smaller breeds and often live less than small breeds.

all, new members join the pack, rankings are gained and lost, old animals are roughly treated by the young ones or even forced to relinquish their position. Perhaps that is so, but since the time that our dogs left the wild, much has happened. Fortunately, our dogs no longer possess all the traits of their wild ancestors, otherwise it would be impossible for them to live with us. And furthermore, we are not wolves, but have developed a certain sense of morality that should also guide us in our attitude toward our (old) dog. For me, that means that I base my decision about whether a second dog is to join us exclusively on the criterion of whether or not it is good for my old dog, and not on selfish concerns or anticipated self-pity.

Older dogs still need love and attention. If you bring another dog home, keep loving your old dog, too.

THE SENIOR YEARS

In times past (hopefully), there were a number of occasions when people parted with their old dogs. The guard dog that no longer could meet the demands of his job, the shepherd dog who no longer had the strength for a whole day's herding work, or the trusty hunting companion whose hunting passion had noticeably diminished were perhaps given away as watch dogs or "released" with a shotgun blast. It was the dog's utility that determined his life. When he no longer could do his work, short shrift was made of him.

Surely, nowadays, that does not happen any more. Most likely, no veterinarian would be willing to euthanize an otherwise healthy dog simply because he is old, but the dog owners of the past, for whom utility was the sole criterion, did not need a veterinarian for this. Nowadays, as a rule, the old utility dog may stay. At least in the case of old service dogs, the handler will usually take his four-legged retiree into his own home if it is at all possible. Retirement in the home of one's old boss certainly must be the most pleasant way to live out his life.

Things have always been different with those dogs that people kept because they enjoyed

As your dog gets older, he'll spend more time sleeping.

Don't be afraid to adopt an old dog. In most cases they are wonderful pets PROVIDING the home from which they came was pleasant for them.

sharing their lives with them. On the one hand, it was understood that there would not be any retirement and there were no questions as to where the dog was to spend his older years. On the other hand, this is one area that provides many opportunities to treat old dogs with extreme cruelty. You all surely know of the many tragedies that may leave a dog without master or mistress—the death of the person to which the dog has bonded, the divorce that leaves no one with enough time for the dog, the illness that makes keeping a dog impossible, and the many inhumanities that people inflict on their trusty friends, such as giving them away when they get old or abandoning them by the side of the road. While a young dog may deal relatively easily with being "expelled" from the familiar pack and joining a new community, such an event will be much more tragic and difficult for an older dog.

But only in the rarest of cases will it be impossible to take in an old dog. Paradoxically, a dog will adapt to a new family or a new human partner more readily if his former home was a good one where mutual affection ruled. Such a dog will mourn, but he almost always will be able to establish a new relationship. After all, during a period of many years he has learned that he can trust people and that a relationship with a person means security and comfort. When such a dog comes to new people, and if these people are not totally unaware of how dogs fit themselves into people's lives, there should be no problems.

It will be entirely different in cases in which an already troubled relationship is terminated once the dog has grown old. There are quite a few so-called breeders who advertise their brood machine for sale once she has become "unserviceable" in order to make a few last bucks from her. The workers in animal shelters could write entire fairy tale books about the reasons why people part with their old dogs. It is always the end of a more or less unhappy relationship between a poor dog and his thoughtless owner. We will not know much about the history of such a dog, but the dog does have a history, a history from which he has learned, and has learned above all how to behave towards people. Living with such a dog can turn out to be very difficult and usually

requires a lot of understanding.

If you want to adopt such a dog, you must be aware that he will behave quite differently at the beginning than he will later. The kind, reserved senior may, after a few months in your care, reveal a combative "Rambo" attitude. Always keep in mind that the previous situation—especially if it was a shelter—made him somewhat insecure. Once he begins to feel at home with you, bad habits and behavior and temperament problems may reveal themselves. There is little you can do to guard against this. Long walks in unfamiliar places or weekend stays at your house are not reliable indicators. All you have on your side are your self-confidence, your intuition, and a large portion of good luck. Such efforts are almost always worthwhile because old dogs are smart dogs and having them as friends is a gift worth fighting for.

ACCLIMATIZATION

It is very important in trying to acclimate your newly acquired senior dog that you know as much as possible about his former life. If you take the dog from a friend because the friend

This old Golden Retriever has a favorite couch to sleep on; he also has his favorite food and his favorite toy or game. If the old dog is new to you, you'll have to learn his likes and dislikes.

can no longer take care of him, such information is easily obtained. You quickly come to know his fears, his likes and dislikes, his tricks when he does not want to do what he is supposed to do, the best way to make him obey, his bad habits and good traits, his favorite meals and what food he does not like at all—all the little things that are important to make your life together a happy one. Make sure to gather all this information, it will come in handy.

In the case of an abandoned senior, no source for such information is available to you. You must become your own private eye, investigating your dog's previous lifestyle. Your task means a lot of observing. Introduce your new old friend to a variety of different situations— take him to the park, let him meet children and adults, and, above all, expose him to other dogs. You will come to know him quickly and thoroughly, but take precautions against unpleasant surprises. Secure your friend with a leash or a long thin nylon lead as long as you are still unsure of his behavior.

Have him perform a number of obedience exercises. This will establish your dominant ranking and, beyond that, will deepen your relationship because everything you do with your dog strengthens the bond between the two of you. Play all the games with him that you and he enjoy. Make this period of acclimatization into a time of joyful getting-to-know-each-other with fun, interest, and, above all, without much fuss. Take your time and give your new friend time and everything will work out.

CHILDREN AND OLD DOGS

In our family photo album there are a lot of pictures that show me as a four- or five-year-old toddler accompanied by a grizzled black hunting spaniel. Mohrle came to us because our neighbor's boss had the opinion that the spaniel was too old for hunting and should be "gotten rid of." Our neighbor asked for the dog, which was generously given to him, and then passed on to us as a playmate.

I do not quite remember if the old fellow turned out to be a playmate or not, but he was a wonderful baby-sitter. He would sit next to us while we played in the sand box and keep watch. He always kept an eye on my sister's stroller and was unhappy when he was called away from guard duty. Mohrle was a friend whose shoulder we could cry on, with whom we could cuddle, and at whose side we could take refreshing naps on the meadow behind the house. Mohrle was too old for rambunctious games, but he was exactly right for the role of older animal "brother."

Something that usually is very difficult to achieve—introducing an old dog, who was unaccustomed to children, into a family with small children—had

Older dogs can still play and be companion animals, but don't expect them to run and jump as well as they did when they were young.

A golden retriever puppy (left) and a mature dog. Goldens can be difficult when they are young. But when they are 2-3 years old they become the most wonderful dogs in terms of intelligence, friendship, work habits and behavior.

worked out well in the case of Mohrle. Mohrle was born to be a baby-sitter. You must not expect this from all dogs. Dogs that are not used to children will often treat them the way they would treat puppies. This means that males will almost always be more tolerant toward the young, and bitches less so. But either will discipline human children the canine way. This will not produce blood, but can be quite painful for a human child without a dog's coat.

If you wish to take in an older dog and you have relatively small children, you must institute a learning program for both. The dog must learn that the children are higher in rank than he is. He will readily accept this as long as the children behave properly. The children must learn that the dog must be respected and that the dog's need for rest must be honored. His basket or resting place should be off limits.

Dogs with little or no experience with children are especially in need of a niche to which they can retreat where no family member will disturb them. Children must learn and understand that the dog is an individual with the right to have his way of life and his needs respected. This is not all that difficult because children demand the same of the family. If there is sufficient time before the arrival of the old dog, you should prepare your children to make their relationship with the dog a happy one. Of course, you will not leave the old dog and your children alone without supervision for the protection of your children, but also for the protection of the dog.

Living with an older dog is an important, and not to be underestimated, life experience for children. They learn that at different ages there are different possibilities of shaping one's life. They understand that consideration and understanding

Dogs with little experience with children must have a place to which they can retreat from the kids and feel safe and secure.

Being old speaks for itself. It's another way of life. It is a winding down process leading to the end.

will enrich their lives together. Children will turn into sensitive observers in order to better understand their canine friends. No one can fully fathom how important it is to a child to be able to cry her heart out at Mohrle's side, or that Mohrle does not care a bit whether others think she is stupid, or whether she is nothing but a bench warmer on the little league team. Mohrle will think his little human friend is the greatest, no matter what the situation.

All kinds of questions are investigated. There is research as to the connection between pet ownership in childhood and the degree of satisfaction with later life. The research can be

An aging Boxer starting to lose his teeth.

An old dog is an old friend.

interpreted to say that satisfaction with one's life, including professional success, increases in direct relation to the emotional bond one has had with dogs. This should not induce us to give dogs as a cure for children with learning problems, but it does make it clear that dogs are of great importance in the maturing process of children.

In this context there is one additional aspect regarding old dogs. Children will experience the sorrowful, though natural, event of a friend's death. In today's society we rarely view death as a part of life. Human death has become a taboo; it usually takes place behind hospital doors and we do not talk about it. This is a shortcoming and a loss, because we desert the dying and are deprived of the insights that understanding our mortality might yield. Dogs, especially old dogs, can be our teachers and help us to find an answer as to what is truly essential in life.

SAYING GOOD-BYE

We all know people who have mourned for their dead dogs. There is also a lack of understanding in people who do not or have not owned a dog. Perhaps you yourself have lost a dog and you know the heaviness of the loss. After he had lived with dogs for 65 years, Konrad Lorenz, the great factual, sensible behaviorist, said, "It is one of the cruelties in this world that the life span of our dogs is so much shorter than ours." The reason for this great sorrow is that we have no other living being that attaches itself to us with such loyalty and unshakable affection, will never betray us, is always there for us, and loves us no matter what.

In the history of the dog/man relationship, there are many testimonials for this close bond and the pain of parting. Nearly every great poet who has owned and loved dogs has written an essay or poem in memory of his dead friend. One of the most beautiful (in my opinion) of these poems is the one by Pablo Neruda, the great, passionate poet of Chile (see p. 56).

(Source: Pablo Neruda. *Late and Posthumous Poems*, 1968-1974. Edited and translated by Ben Belitt. Grove Press: New York, 1988)

Poems and stories are memorials for dogs. In addition to those literary mementos there have been real monuments for dogs. Many of you may be familiar with the story of the faithful Akita in Japan who went to the railroad station every day to meet his master. When his master stopped arriving by train, because he had died, the faithful dog continued to go to the station every afternoon hoping to greet his master. Today there stands a statue at the place

A pet cemetery.

NEAR THIS SPOT ARE DEPOSITED THE
REMAINS OF ONE WHO POSSESSED
BEAUTY WITHOUT VANITY
STRENGTH WITHOUT INSOLENCE
COURAGE WITHOUT FEROCITY
AND ALL THE VIRTUES OF MAN
WITHOUT HIS VICES

My dog's dead.

I buried him in the garden near the wreck
of some rusting machinery.

There, neither aboveground
nor underneath, in due course
he'll come to my whistle.
For the present he has taken his fine mop of hair,
his bad education, his cold nose, somewhere else.
And I, a materialist, with no faith
in the sky's apocalyptical promises
to departed humanity——
for this dog and the rest of all dogdom I
believe in heaven: yes, I believe in a heaven
I will never enter myself—but there he'll be waiting,
thumping his tail like a fan
to confirm our old friendship, in the event that I do.
Well—let's not talk of grief here upon earth,
where I no longer can have a companion
who was never my flunky.
What we had was a porcupine's friendship
that kept his own distance,
the fellowship of a star independently fixed,
with only a functional intimacy
that spurned all excesses.
He never pawed over my wardrobe
or plagued me with dog hairs and mange,
never rubbed his behind on my knees
with a dog's sexual obsession.
No. my dog faced me fairly

with precisely the attention I needed—-
the solitude due
a vainglorious man to make clear
that, being a dog,
he was wasting his time
bestowing a gaze with a look
that reserved all its sweetness for me: all that
hairy existence, that taciturn life
always close, with no petty annoyances,
no expectation of benefit.

How I loved to trail after, to
meander the Black Island beaches
alongside him in winter's great solitude.
Overhead, a sky crisscrossed
by glacial birds, up in front, my dog
dashing off as he pleased, hirsute, full of
watery voltage in motion:
my vagabond, olfactory dog
spreading his tail like a pennant, aglow
with the gilded encounter of Ocean and spume.

Happiness, happiness, happiness—-
the dog's doggy felicity
never more nor less than itself, with the absolute
fullness of impudent nature.

No goodbyes for a dead dog.
And no lies. We never lied to each other.

He is gone and I buried him. There's an end of it.

-Pablo Neruda (from *Late and Posthumous Poems*, 1968-1974. Grove Press: New York, 1988.)

where he used to wait, a symbol of faithfulness.

The famous Lord Byron had a monument erected for his Newfoundland, Botswain. The inscription on the plaque of the tombstone in the park of New Steat Abbey reads:

(Source: Brackert/Kleffens, 1989)

We know of memorials for dogs as far back as Roman antiquity, such as the mausoleums that the Roman emperor Hadrian (76—138 AD) had built for his dogs. Friedrich II, King of Prussia,

---

𝕹ear this spot are deposited the remains of one

who possessed beauty without vanity,

strength without insolence, courage without ferocity,

and all the virtues of man without his vices.

This praise, which would be unmeaning flattery

if inscribed over human ashes,

is but a just tribute

to the memory of 𝕭otswain, a dog,

who was born in 𝕹ewfoundland 𝕸ay 1803

and died at 𝕹ewsteat 𝕹ovember 18, 1808.

(Source: *Byron's Letters and Journals*, Vol. 1: 1798-1810. Edited by Leslie A. Marchand. Belknap Press of Harvard University Press: Cambridge, 1973. p. 176.)

Tombstones and monuments for dogs have been around for a long time. Some emphasize the practical value of the dog, as, for example, this tombstone inscription from the 17th century that will make you smile:

The thieves I charged, the lovers I let be

Thus was done the master's will and that of the ladies.

Getting down the steps becomes more and more difficult as your dog gets older.

Dog plots are marked in many ways at a dog cemetery.

(1712—1786 AD), followed the same practice. In his last will and testament, Old Fritz decreed that he wanted to be laid to rest in a mausoleum surrounded by the graves of his favorite dogs. It took more than 200 years until finally, in 1991, Old Fritz's wish was done.

The common man, too, soon began erecting memorials for his darlings—they run the gamut from simple grave markers to "room-mausoleums" containing the ashes of the dead dog. A special form of memorial is provided by taxidermy, that is, the stuffing and mounting of the animal. In the 19th century, this became the fashion all over Europe. The most famous stuffed dog, without a doubt, is found in the Museum of Natural History in Bern, Switzerland. Barry is the hero from the Augustine monastery at the Great St. Bernard mountain pass who is said to have saved the lives of 40 people and died during his 41st rescue attempt when a soldier of Napoleon's beaten army stabbed him to death by mistake.

I am glad that this fashion has fallen out of favor, but our times also have their own strange fads. For instance, some people will pay over $1,000 for a burial at sea for their dog. The burial business for pets is booming. Dog cemeteries have become eloquent testimonies to the modern form of worshipping the dead.

How to remember one's dog is a matter of taste. As long as good taste and the rights of others are preserved, each person should be able to experience his own way of mourning. The important thing is that every dog owner, when parting from his dog, should conduct himself with respect and dignity.

EUTHANASIA: AN ACT OF MERCY AND COURAGE

One morning, my friend Inge came downstairs and found her old dog Bora in her basket as if asleep—she had died during the night. Jeff the Husky, old and seriously ill, woke his master in the night and led him into the cool basement, where he liked to spend the hot summer days. Once they had arrived there, Jeff lay down, expelled one breath, and died.

Most dog owners wish for such a parting. They want their friend to pass away peacefully and in familiar surroundings. But only a few dog owners will be granted such a farewell. Usually there will be an ailment at the end that demands a decision. Such a decision is always a difficult one because we cannot stop hoping. We tend to deceive ourselves, and we simply do not wish to part with our dog.

Most dog owners that I know do not regret that they had their old dogs put to sleep in order to spare themselves inconveniences, but rather that it took them "too long" to gather the courage to make the decision. Frequently, we will need the advice from friends or from a veterinarian who can tell us when we act or not act out of misplaced love.

Discuss with your veterinarian the following questions and observe your own reactions:

What is the prognosis for my dog?

Is it possible to keep my dog free of pain and does he still enjoy life?

Am I prepared and capable of providing proper care for my dog?

Will my family support the decision?

When you and the veterinarian agree that it would be better for the dog to be put to sleep, do not hesitate. You are not "killing" your dog. It is your right and your duty to make the best decision for him. It can be a great act of mercy for our dogs if we spare them predictable fear, pain, and suffering.

Keep in mind that your dog lives only in the present. He does not know what happened in the past and cannot trust in the future. He is doing poorly now and he is suffering now. He cannot recall the good times that you shared and find comfort in these memories. He lives in the present, experiencing all his joy of life and all his suffering as it happens. Keep this in mind and exercise your privilege to have him put to sleep in the interest of your dog, even if you find it so very difficult. You owe it to your dog.

When a dog dies, unlike with the death of a person, there is one possible comfort—you can get a new dog. If you wish to continue sharing your life with a dog, do not put off looking for a successor. He will be a different dog than his predecessor, but he will become the same kind of friend that the old dog was to you. You are not unfaithful to your old friend if you acquire a new dog quickly. Rather, you are honoring his memory and the unique bond between dog and man.

For many, the pet/owner bond goes beyond simple companionship; pets are often considered members of the family. A leading pet food manufacturer recently conducted a nationwide survey of pet owners to gauge just how important pets were in their lives. Here's what they found:

- 76 percent allow their pets to sleep on their beds
- 78 percent think of their pets as their children
- 84 percent display photos of their pets, mostly in their homes
- 84 percent think that their pets react to their own emotions
- 100 percent talk to their pets
- 97 percent think that their pets understand what they're saying

Are you surprised?

WHEN DOES MY DOG REQUIRE GERIATRIC OBSERVATION?

Inasmuch as the aging process varies as much with dogs as with humans, when your dog should start geriatric care will vary. The following chart is a suggestion as to when you should remind your veterinarian that you have an aging dog.

- Dogs which weigh less than 50 pounds: 9 years
- Dogs which are from 51 to 90 pounds: 7 years
- Dogs which are heavier than 90 pounds: 6 years

A good veterinarian should be responsible for your dog from the time you select the puppy best suited to your lifestyle and pocketbook, till you need bereavement counseling upon the death of your dog.

Diseases which are common to older dogs are:
- Anemia
- Cancer
- Cataracts
- Cardiovascular disease
- Chronic renal disease
- Degenerative bone disease
- Diabetes
- Hepatopathies
- Hyperadrenocorticism
- Hypertension
- Hypothyroidism
- Keratoconjunctivitis sicca
- Obesity
- Orodental disease
- Prostatic disease
- Urinary incontinence
- Urolithiasi